GEISTLICHE HARMONIEN III

Collegium Musicum: Yale University
Leon Plantinga and James Grier, general editors

COLLEGIUM MUSICUM, a series of publications of the Yale University Department of Music, was initiated by the late Leo Schrade in 1955. Since 1969 the series has been published by A-R Editions, Inc., with selection of materials and establishment of editorial policy the responsibility of the Yale music faculty. The aim of COLLEGIUM MUSICUM: YALE UNIVERSITY, in its second series, remains that set forth by Professor Schrade in the very first volume: to "present compositions which, through neglect or lack of knowledge, have been ungraciously forgotten or overlooked, despite their artistic value and historical importance."

Subscribers to this series, as well as patrons of subscribing institutions, are invited to apply for information about the "Copyright-Sharing Policy" of A-R Editions, Inc., under which the contents of this volume may be reproduced free of charge for study or performance.

For information contact A-R EDITIONS, INC.
                  801 Deming Way
                  Madison, Wisconsin 53717

First Series

1. Alessandro Scarlatti: PASSIO D. N. JESU CHRISTI SECUNDUM JOHANNEM. Edited by Edwin Hanley.
2. THIRTY CHANSONS FOR THREE AND FOUR VOICES FROM ATTAINGNANT's COLLECTIONS. Edited by Albert Seay.
3. Michael Haydn: TE DEUM IN C (1770). Edited by Reinhard G. Pauly.
4. THE WICKHAMBROOK LUTE MANUSCRIPT. Edited by Daphne E. R. Stephens.
5. MISSAE CAPUT. Edited by Alejandro Enrique Planchart.
6. THIRTY-FIVE CONDUCTUS FOR TWO AND THREE VOICES. Edited by Janet Knapp.

Second Series

1. Antonio Cesti: FOUR CHAMBER DUETS. Edited by David L. Burrows.
2. Carl Philipp Emanuel Bach: HARPSICHORD CONCERTO IN D MAJOR, W. 27. Edited by Elias N. Kulukundis.
3. Johann Mattheson: DAS LIED DES LAMMES. Edited by Beekman C. Cannon.
4. ENGLISH PASTIME MUSIC, 1630–1660. Edited by Martha Maas.
5. Carl Heinrich Graun: DER TOD JESU. Edited by Howard Serwer.
6. Franz Johann Habermann: MISSA SANCTI WENCESLAI, MARTYRIS. Edited by William D. Gudger.
7. Christoph Schaffrath: CONCERTO IN B-FLAT FOR CEMBALO AND STRINGS. Edited by Karyl Louwenaar.
8. LIBRO PRIMO DE LA CROCE. Edited by William F. Prizer.
9. Felix Mendelssohn Bartholdy: O HAUPT VOLL BLUT UND WUNDEN. Edited by R. Larry Todd.
10. Biagio Marini: STRING SONATAS FROM OPUS 1 AND OPUS 8. Edited by Thomas D. Dunn.
11. FESTIVE TROPED MASSES FROM THE ELEVENTH CENTURY: CHRISTMAS AND EASTER IN THE QUITAINE. *Puer natus est* Mass and *Resurrexi* Mass reconstructed and transcribed by Charlotte Roederer.
12. Antonio Sartorio: GIULIO CESARE IN EGITTO. Edited by Craig Monson.
13. Samuel Capricornus: GEISTLICHE HARMONIEN III. Edited by Paul Walker.

COLLEGIUM MUSICUM: YALE UNIVERSITY • SECOND SERIES • VOLUME 13

Samuel Capricornus

GEISTLICHE HARMONIEN III

Edited by Paul Walker

 A-R Editions, Inc.

Madison

ISBN 0-89579-380-6
ISSN 0147-0108

♾ The paper used in this publication meets the minimum requirements of
the American National Standard for Information Sciences—Permanence of
Paper for Printed Library Materials, ANSI Z39.48-1984.

Contents

Acknowledgments

I wish first of all to thank The Friends of Music at Yale, in particular Elias N. Kulukundis, for providing funds to hire clerical assistance. I also wish to thank Leon Plantinga for first inviting me to contribute to the *Collegium Musicum: Yale University* series and to recognize him and James Grier for their efforts and advice in the editorial phases of the project. Acknowledgment is further due to students Jessica Johnson and Penelope Ward for initially inputting the music into the computer and saving me countless hours. Finally, it will have been the greatest reward for my labors if scholars and performers should find the works contained herein worthy of both study and public performance.

Introduction

To know baroque music today is in most cases to know the innovative works of its earliest masters (Monteverdi and Schütz) and the transcendent masterpieces of its final flowering (principally Bach, Handel, and Vivaldi). With a very few notable exceptions (one might name Corelli's Christmas Concerto, a few of Buxtehude's organ praeludia, and Purcell's *Dido and Aeneas*) the music in between has, aside from the occasional performance, languished forgotten and ignored. Into this void fall a great many fine compositions by a great many first-rate composers, perhaps none more unjustly neglected than Samuel Capricornus, kapellmeister first to the city of Pressburg (Bratislava) and later to the Württemberg court in Stuttgart. Although scarcely one in twenty musicologists today can place the name in any context at all, Capricornus was in his day a central figure of the generation after Schütz: he admired and mastered the contemporary Italian styles as practiced by Carissimi and the Vienna court kapellmeisters Giovanni Valentini and Antonio Bertali; he wrote excellent music in which those styles were integrated with the traditions established for Lutheran Germany by Schütz and Schein; and he worked ceaselessly to introduce the new music both through its performance and through publication and wide distribution of his own compositions. Capricornus's few known works for the stage are lost (as are those of Schütz), but he published over a dozen collections of vocal and instrumental ensemble music of high quality at a time when few composers saw their works in print. These volumes formed a part of nearly every important choir library and private collection in late-seventeenth-century Germany, including that of Buxtehude in the Marienkirche in Lübeck and the Lüneburg choir school where J. S. Bach was a student. One cannot fully understand the evolution of German sacred music between Schütz and Bach without some acquaintance with the works of Samuel Capricornus.

It is all the more unfortunate, therefore, that most of Capricornus's compositions remain unavailable today in any format but the original partbooks.[1] The present edition aims to remedy this oversight by offering an entire collection from the composer's mature years, the *Geistliche Harmonien III* of 1664. It is my hope that both scholars and performers will thereby be stimulated to learn more about this undeservedly neglected composer and his era in the history of Western music.

Biography

The known facts of Capricornus's biography are relatively straightforward. He was born Samuel Bockshorn (Latin: Capricornus) in 1628 into the family of a Lutheran pastor in the small town of Schertitz (now Zercice, near Mloda Boleslav, currently in the Czech Republic). His childhood must have been difficult if not traumatic. Zercice was completely destroyed in the Thirty Years' War, the family moved to Hungary to avoid religious persecution, and Capricornus's father died young, so that the young Samuel traveled widely before taking his first important position in 1651 as civic music director and teacher of Latin in Pressburg (Czech: Bratislava, currently in Slovakia), not far east of Vienna. Nothing is known of Capricornus's musical training, but he proved to be a tenacious and tireless champion of modern (i.e., contemporary Italian) music, especially the works of Carissimi and the Italians resident in Vienna. Capricornus is known to have been in Vienna in 1649–50 as a member of the imperial chapel and to have met Valentini shortly before the latter died in 1649. One can gain some sense of his Italian bent by learning that Carissimi's oratorio *Judicio Salamonis* was after Capricornus's death erroneously included as his in a published collection (*Continuo Theatri musici*, 1669) devoted to his works.

Capricornus's first published collection, which appeared in 1655, shows at once a preference for the kind of large-scale concerted works in Venetian style provided for the Viennese court by Valentini and for the Saxon court by Schütz. In fact, Capricornus sent a copy of the collection to Schütz, who declared himself "delighted" by the work.[2] Carissimi paid Capricornus the compliment of performing in St. Apollinare a composition that Capricornus had sent to him. Although in Bratislava Capricornus had a relatively large performing ensemble at his disposal, and although the position kept him close to Vienna, he resigned it in 1657 "for reasons of health" and accepted an offer to serve as court kapellmeister to the duke of Württemberg in Stuttgart.[3]

It is easy to imagine what might have attracted Capricornus to this post. The Württemberg court boasted a tradition of musical patronage that included among its pre-war kapellmeisters the composer Leonhard Lechner and among its famous sons the keyboard master Johann Jacob Froberger.[4] Furthermore, the diversity of Stuttgart's musical program rivaled that of the most prestigious German courts. Large-scale theatrical productions with music could be mounted in its world-renowned Pleasure Palace (*Lusthaus*), a large and elaborately-decorated theater built in the 1580s according to French designs. An active *Kammermusik* had been developed by the English lutenist John Price, who spent the years 1605–25 in the employ of the Württemberg dukes. Not least of all, the dukes apparently paid their musicians faithfully, at a time when the musicians of the Saxon court in Dresden frequently found it necessary to petition for back pay. It is also possible that Capricornus's decision may have been influenced in part by Württemberg's importance as a stronghold of Protestantism.

The Württemberg court must have been very pleased to snare as kapellmeister a prominent composer from near the imperial capital city who was well versed in the contemporary Italian styles. The Thirty Years' War had seriously curtailed the court's ability to maintain any sort of musical establishment, especially after the massive invasion of foreign troops that followed the battle of Nördlingen in 1634. The rebuilding of the Württemberg musical establishment had begun only four years before Capricornus answered the call, and the reigning Duke Eberhard III must surely have thought that the glorious days of old were about to return. The number of musicians at the new kapellmeister's disposal remained relatively modest, but mid-century Italian trends (away from the Venetian polychoral style and toward the more intimate settings for solo, duet, and trio with basso continuo and perhaps a pair of violins) fit these circumstances well. In fact, most of Capricornus's later compositions reflect the stylistic shift toward fewer performers and more affective expression.

In spite of all the promising signs, Capricornus's years in Stuttgart proved to be neither happy nor long-lived. He arrived to find a local musician, the court organist Philipp Friedrich Böddecker, resentful for having been passed over for the post, and the two men seem to have clashed almost immediately. Within half a year Capricornus wrote a long, detailed, and heated letter defending himself against various charges, of which the most interesting to us today (and the least personal) involve certain criticisms of the new Italian style of composition.[5] Like the Danzig organist Paul Siefert earlier in the century and Giovanni Maria Artusi at its beginning, Böddecker decried the barbarities of modern music and cited specific examples of incorrect part-writing and voice leading to argue his case. Capricornus's detailed response offers us a valuable glimpse into a musical style in transition; that is, a style still based on counterpoint but trying to sort out for itself which of the

sixteenth-century Zarlinian rules were still valid and which had been rendered obsolete by new ideals of melody, texture, instrumentation, and textual expression. Present-day musicians for whom Bach represents the pinnacle of baroque style will, for instance, be surprised to see Capricornus defend the presence of parallel perfect consonances by citing examples from the works of Valentini and Bertali, much as Brahms was later to do from works of Beethoven and others.[6]

Additional criticism of the new kapellmeister's great demands on the court instrumentalists and singers suggests that Capricornus held his performers to high standards and was demanding in rehearsals. Among their complaints were that he pushed them to play in the upper ranges of their instruments, that he insisted they play other sizes of instruments in the same family, and in one case that he caused Böddecker's brother, normally a cornettist, to sing "so high that it caused him physical weakness, shortness of breath, and the reduction of his vocal capacity by half, with no possibility of ever regaining it fully."[7] Capricornus for his part complained that the cornettists blew their instruments "like cowhorns" and that they drank too much. A panel appointed by Duke Eberhard to investigate the charges found for the most part in favor of the kapellmeister, but they advised him to treat his subordinates more gently (*mit Glimpf*). Nor was Capricornus's personal life without its storminess: in 1662 he petitioned the duke to settle a marital dispute.

Capricornus died in 1665 at the age of only thirty-seven. He left behind a significant body of work that included ten published collections of sacred music (three of which appeared posthumously), three of madrigals and other secular vocal works, and three of instrumental compositions.[8] His successor as kapellmeister continued to complain about the unruliness and lack of discipline among the court musicians, and the program appears to have remained mired in controversy until the hiring in 1700 of J. Sigismund Kusser.

Geistliche Harmonien III

The pieces of *Geistliche Harmonien III* belong to the category of small sacred concerto: brief works for small numbers of voices, obbligato instruments, and continuo, set to prose texts generally taken from the Bible (or imitative of the Biblical style) or of a devotional, prayer-like nature. The texts project a variety of characters (theological, private/devotional, pictorial) and moods (supplicatory, sensual, joyful, militant, humble), and Capricornus matches these with a comparable variety of musical means and effects. We find suave Italianate melodic writing, disarmingly simple one moment, beautifully embellished the next, side-by-side with more instrumentally-conceived German-style vocal lines. Although solo passages can be found in nearly every piece, Capricornus cannot hide his German love for counterpoint, and the myriad combinations of singers and instruments create ever fresh and interesting textures. Also suggestive of the composer's German heritage is his extensive and creative use of instruments, especially winds (recorder, cornetto, bassoon, trombone) as well as viola da gamba and occasionally violas. Among the artistic highlights of the collection are the sensuous "Ich bin schwarz" with its colorful combination of high and low sonorities; the vigorous "Es stehe Gott auf" with its virtuoso bassoon solos; the jubilant "Singet Gott" with its rollicking compound meter; the sonorous "Ad te suspiro" with its six-part string accompaniment; and the sweet "Dulcis amor" with its Italianate vocal lines and darker accompaniment for two violas. For virtuosity, "Kommet her, ihr Völker," characterized by rapid vocal passagework evocative of thunder, earthquakes, the scattering of peoples, and rising to heaven, would be difficult to surpass.

Matters of Performance

Basso Continuo

As more students of baroque music acquire facility in thoroughbass realization, editors grow less inclined to realize these parts for performers. Experienced players know that the process of "unrealizing" a written-out continuo part, that is, trying *not* to play what appears on the page, can be a frustrating one. Furthermore, no two performances of a given piece will be accompanied exactly the same. A myriad of factors enter into continuo players' overall conception of their accompaniment as well as many of the moment-by-moment decisions that they make in the performance: the particular qualities of the soloist(s) being accompanied, the particular instrument played, the size of the room and its acoustical properties. For all of these reasons, and, not least, because Capricornus's thoroughbass parts are in the main not terribly difficult to realize, I have chosen not to write out such a part.

This is not to say that the modern player faces no difficulties in working out accompaniments to these pieces. Capricornus stands at the threshold of the tradition of tonal writing familiar to us in the works of Corelli, Vivaldi, Bach, and Handel. His handling of chord progression approaches in many respects this later style but retains certain quirks that betray its indebtedness to older contrapuntal models. As a result, players trained in the Bach/Handel style will encounter progressions for which their training has

not prepared them. A second difficulty, which exacerbates the first, is that Capricornus's bass, while rather generously figured, is not quite sufficiently figured to supply the player with absolutely all necessary information. It is well known that Italian composers of the period preferred to leave their basses largely unfigured and expected the players to work out their own accompaniments. Capricornus's basses omit enough necessary information to suggest that he likewise expected his continuo players to use a certain amount of common sense. Common sense derived from eighteenth-century harmonic practice, however, will not always lead the player to sound judgments for the pieces in *Geistliche Harmonien III*.

To assist the player, therefore, in producing a stylistically proper accompaniment, I have added a substantial number of figures (indicated with square brackets) offering my best understanding of Capricornus's approach to chord progression. In many cases, these added figures simply record the harmonies produced by the various parts above the bass. In others, however, Capricornus leaves the issue in doubt and the editor or player is forced to decide. For instance, because a student of figured bass today is taught to play a root-position triad above any unfigured note, all unfigured Es should "properly" signify E-minor triads (there being no piece in *Geistliche Harmonien III* that includes G-sharp in its key signature). Sometimes, however, Capricornus's parts above such an unfigured bass note spell a C-major first-inversion triad. Complicating the player's decision for a given E is Capricornus's penchant in full textures for restricting all upper parts to the notes E and G, with neither a B nor a C to be found. In fact, this phenomenon occurs frequently enough to suggest that the continuo player might choose to play only octaves, thirds, and tenths above such an ambiguous bass note. In these cases, however, I have elected to suggest which triad seems to fit better the composer's overall style.

A further difficulty of Capricornus's harmony involves what we might, using today's vocabulary, refer to as secondary dominant chords and leading tones. If we return to the problematic unfigured E, we may note that sometimes the upper parts spell an E-major chord despite the absence of a sharp below the bass note. When no upper parts offer guidance, however, how does one decide whether to play a major or a minor chord? This decision is a judgment call. Another troublesome issue arises in pieces with "incomplete signatures," especially those in "C minor" with only one flat in the signature. In such a case, one most often puzzles over the use of the lowered sixth scale degree, A-flat. In particular, should the chord above F (the modern subdominant) be major or minor? Editors and players have in the past been perhaps too cautious in their adding of accidentals. This caution is understandable as an antidote to editorial practice in which "primitive" harmonies were sometimes "improved" to conform to later practice, and it would be unwise to abandon it completely. Nevertheless, as we become more familiar with the music of Monteverdi, Schütz, Carissimi, and many others among Capricornus's contemporaries and immediate predecessors, we become bolder in supplying editorial accidentals. I have tried to use sound but careful judgment in all such cases. As seventeenth-century harmony is studied in greater detail, perhaps the scholarly community will some day soon be able to offer more secure guidelines.

One particular element of Capricornus's harmonic practice that deserves special mention is what today's musicians refer to, disapprovingly, as the regression: the chord progression involving root movement down by step. Avoidance of parallel perfect consonances is especially nettlesome in such cases, but Capricornus himself offers a way around this difficulty. The opening section of "Ach lieber Herr" abounds with slow descending scalar passages in both bass and principal theme. These he accompanies with an eight-note figure that consistently changes the root-position chord to first inversion before the next chord is struck. In this way both awkward melodic motion and parallel perfect consonances are avoided. I (and apparently the composer as well) encourage the player to make liberal use of this "trick."

These several difficulties are counterbalanced by certain characteristics that make Capricornus's basses simple and fun to realize even for the amateur or unpracticed. One such characteristic is the relative absence of seventh chords. Capricornus employs the seventh almost exclusively in its traditional sixteenth-century role as part of the 7-6 progression (which is best realized $\frac{7}{3}$ rather than $\frac{7}{5}$). The chords $\frac{6}{5}$, $\frac{4}{3}$, and $\frac{4}{2}$ appear infrequently, however. The basis of the harmony therefore remains that of the sixteenth-century motet sound: pure triads. This fact, coupled with the rarity of $\frac{6}{4}$ chords, means that the player is playing simple root-position and first-inversion triads (with the traditional suspensions 4-3, 2-3, and 2-1) nearly all the time. The absence of common-practice (i.e., Bachian) tonal harmony, combined with the relative brevity of the pieces, also means that the prospect of modulation is almost entirely absent. Although the use of accidentals is less predictable (some might say less logical) than in later tonal music, one need not face the prospect of a complete conceptual leap to a new tonal area halfway through a piece.

Finally, continuo players trained on Bach and Handel may have difficulty adapting to an aesthetic in which the avoidance of parallel perfect consonances and of doubling other vocal and instrumental parts is considerably less important than in later music. The less-experienced player, on the other hand, may breathe a sigh of relief. Capricornus himself went on record with a defense of parallel fifths when he was accused by Böddecker of contrapuntal clumsiness.[9] He cited in his defense examples by many of the leading Italian composers of the day, and one can indeed find rather bald or thinly-veiled examples in the present collection. (For an example of the former, see "Ad te suspiro," m. 48, violins 1 and 2; for the latter, see "Ich bin eine Blume zu Saron," mm. 38–39, violin 1, alto, and basso continuo.) Because musicians since the baroque period have tended to view Handel and Bach as its leading practitioners, and because the true purpose of most figured-bass exercises as taught today is to instill rigor in the writing of counterpoint and the handling of voice leading, it is easy to forget that one of the principal impulses behind the idea of the basso continuo was the desire to loosen music from the contrapuntal strictures of Zarlino and Palestrina. As such reformers as Vincenzo Galilei saw it, counterpoint had become an impediment to drama and expression.

Of course, there was a second, contemporaneous impulse behind the creation of basso continuo texture that stood almost in opposition to this dissatisfaction with intricate counterpoint. For Ludovico Viadiana, a basso continuo part allowed the organist to supply those intricate inner parts when only one or two soloists had to take the place of the more usual motet choir. One might reasonably expect seventeenth-century sacred music, therefore, to require a strictly-worked-out, motet-style accompaniment, whereas the accompanist of a secular cantata or opera would be expected to aim for a more flexible, less "busy" style that followed every nuance of the soloist. As anyone familiar with music of the period knows, however, lines dividing the two are nearly impossible to draw. Certainly Capricornus wanted his church pieces to be expressive. He chose texts that were seldom liturgical but frequently dramatic or colorful, took pains to ensure that his music brought out the sense of the words, and included a great many solo passages accompanied only by continuo. In short, the person who realizes the figured basses in this collection may in good conscience concentrate more on expressive accompanying and somewhat less on contrapuntal rigor than would be prudent for Bach or Handel.

In his book on continuo playing in Schütz, Gerhard Kirchner recommends the use of only three voices, rather than four as is frequently taught, in accompanying solo singing of the period.[10] This suggestion also works well for Capricornus's music.

When the texture is fuller, on the other hand, four or even more voices will likely be preferable. I offer below two samples of my own continuo realization, both from "Ad te suspiro": Example 1 illustrates the beginning of this piece, where the full texture of five independent instrumental parts calls for a full-voiced sound in the accompaniment; Example 2, the opening of the first vocal section, where the player must accompany first a soprano soloist, then a bass. Most thoroughbass manuals today recommend keeping the right hand in a somewhat low range, below the soloist when possible, but in any case generally in an alto/tenor range. This avoids drawing too much attention to the accompaniment and is my recommendation as well. When the soloist is a bass (or perhaps tenor), however, the continuo part will naturally be more easily heard. In this case, players should be less concerned about how high they play and should think more carefully about creating an interesting top line that forms good counterpoint with the soloist's part.

The most proper instrument for continuo realization of church music is the organ, and fortunate is the performer who has a small positive organ or well-placed, well-voiced tracker on which to accompany these pieces. Players and scholars have in the last few years come to show much greater flexibility in their use of continuo instruments than was formerly the case. It is no longer thought, for instance, that some sort of low melodic instrument is always necessary for doubling the bass line. Indeed, *Geistliche Harmonien III* offers additional evidence against this thinking. One could argue that Capricornus has in fact supplied just such a low melodic part, somewhat independent of the regular continuo part, when and only when he wanted one. I am inclined to leave to performers the question of what instruments to use in realizing Capricornus's continuo parts. One combination that has found particular favor recently among performers is that of organ with theorbo, a combination explicitly mentioned by Johann Hermann Schein in the introduction to his *Musica Nova II*.[11] Certainly an organ is by itself sufficient for all of the pieces in the present volume, but a good one may not always be available, and baroque composers and performers were rather less dogmatic about the single and only way to perform a piece of music than Western musicians since the nineteenth century have become.

Performing Forces

The *Capella* during Capricornus's tenure in Stuttgart was never large.[12] Whereas before the Thirty Years' War it had numbered thirty-one singers plus instrumentalists, at the time of publication of *Geist-*

liche Harmonien III, it comprised a total of only twenty-two members, including singers, instrumentalists, kapellmeister, and organist. An undated list of chapel personnel from Capricornus's tenure names only five singers: two boy sopranos and one each male alto, tenor, and bass. Instruments mentioned on this list include cornetto, sackbut, violin, flute, viola da gamba, trumpet, kettle drums, and organ. Many performers played more than one instrument. Based on both this information and the musical style of *Geistliche Harmonien III*, there can be little doubt that the composer would have expected these pieces to be performed with only one singer or player per part.

Regarding instruments, modern performers are nowadays quite familiar with the baroque versions of the instruments named by Capricornus, and nothing further need be said about them. The only difficulty in instrumentation might perhaps arise in realizing the five recorder parts (originally labeled "flutes") of "Ich bin schwarz." Using modern instruments pitched in C and F, these might most readily be distributed as two sopranos, alto, alto/tenor, and tenor. These parts have been notated in clefs to which modern recorder players are generally accustomed and will of course sound an octave higher than notated.

Pulse and Flow

Performers are reminded that the barlines in this edition serve simply to keep the parts lined up properly in a score rather than to indicate to performers a place for heavy emphasis. Of course, barlines do also serve to regulate the underlying flow (pulse, if you will) of the harmonies.[13] Nevertheless, a great deal of the musical interest in this style comes about because the individual parts do NOT slavishly proceed according to this pulse. In short, the barlines are placed principally to facilitate rehearsal and performance, not principally to inform stylistic interpretation. I recommend a moderate half-note rather than a quick quarter-note pulse in order to aid the flow of the music.

Pitch

"Ich weiß, daß der Herr" includes both a low C for the bass and a high A for the first soprano. This composite vocal range suggests (at least given the nature of modern voices) a pitch level rather close to A 440.

Instrumentation of "Anima mea"

The table of contents in the basso continuo partbook indicates two violin parts for "Anima mea," but there is no "Violino II" part to be found and the title is omitted from the Instrumentum Secundum partbook. Furthermore, in the Instrumentum Primum partbook the piece is headed simply "Violino," just

Example 1. "Ad te suspiro," mm. 1–5, with realization of figured bass.

Example 2. "Ad te suspiro," mm. 11–27, with realization of figured bass.

as it is for "Præparate," where there is only one violin part, instead of "Violino I" as it is for all pieces with two violin parts. Since, furthermore, the piece sounds complete as it stands, the indication of two violin parts in the table of contents is presumed to be an oversight.

Notes

1. The only works presently available in modern edition are the complete *Opus musicum* (1655) (Bratislava: Opus, 1975), ed. R. Rybaric, and excerpts from *Jubilus Bernhardi* (1660) in the master's thesis by S. Sametz, *The "Jubilus Bernardi" of Samuel Capricornus* (University of Wisconsin, 1980). A recently released compact disc (Opus 111 label, no. OPS 30–99, issued 1994) offers selections from *Lieder des Leyden und Tode Jesu, Scelta Musicale,* and *Theatrum Musicum* in performances by Le Parlement de Musique directed by Martin Gester.

2. "Deß Herrn *opera virtuosa* . . . hat mich sehr *delectirt.*" Quoted in Joseph Sittard, "Samuel Capricornus contra Philipp Friedrich Böddecker," *Sammelbände der internationalen Musikgesellschaft* 3 (1901–2): 92.

3. On Capricornus's years in Pressburg, see Richard Rybaric, "Samuel Capricornus in Bratislava/Pressburg," *Musica Antique III: Musica Scientifica* (Bydgoszcz, Poland: Bydgoskie Towarzystwo Naurkowe, 1972), 107–26 (in German).

4. Further information on the history of music at the Württemberg court can be found in Josef Sittard, *Zur Geschichte der Musik und des Theaters am Württembergischen Hofe,* 2 vols. (Stuttgart: W. Kohlhammer, 1890; reprinted as 1 vol., Hildesheim: Georg Olms, 1970).

5. Completely transcribed, with discussion, in Sittard, "Capricornus contra Böddecker," 87–128.

6. For Capricornicus's arguments, see particularly Sittard, "Capricornus contra Böddecker," 96–105. Brahms's list of parallel fifths can be found in Paul Mast, "Brahms's Study, *Octaven u. Quinten u. A.,* with Schenker's Commentary Translated," *Music Forum* 5 (1980): 1–196.

7. Quoted by Sametz, *The "Jubilus Bernardi,"* p. 5 and n. 15.

8. For a complete inventory of the extant sacred works for three or more voices, see Diane Parr Walker and Paul Walker, *German Sacred Polyphonic Vocal Music Between Schütz and Bach* (Warren, Michigan: Harmonie Park Press, 1992), 114–20.

9. See note 5 above.

10. G. Kirchner, *Der Generalbaß bei Heinrich Schütz* (Kassel: Bärenreiter, 1960), 50–55.

11. "So habe ich nur dieses hierbey einfellichen, wann in einem oder dem andern meiner *Concertlein* etwa eine Stimme nur alleine singet, es dahin angesehen, daß der *Bassus Continuus,* nebenst deme daß er auff der Orgel, Positif oder Regal, miteingeschlagen wird, auch uberdas noch für eine oder mehr Lautten, Teorben, Pandorn und andere dergleichen beseitete vollstimmigte Instrumenta, welche dann solcher alleine singenden und zimlich blos kommenden Stim, voraus in grossen Kirchen, eine gute *assistentz* leisten, und ein freundliches Geleidt geben können, müsse abgeschrieben, und darauff mitgespielet werden." For a facsimile, see Johann Hermann Schein, *Neue Ausgabe sämtlicher Werke, vol. 5: Opella Nova II, 1626* (Kassel: Bärenreiter, 1986), xiv.

12. This information is taken from Sametz *The "Jubilus Bernardi,"* 20–23, which is in turn taken from H. Buchner, *Samuel Friedrich Capricornus* (Dissertation, University of Munich, 1922).

13. See, for instance, Gioseffo Zarlino, *Le istitutioni harmoniche,* chapter 48, "The Measure," in *The Art of Counterpoint,* trans. Guy A. Marco and Claude Palisca (New Haven: Yale University Press, 1968), 116–20.

Texts and Translations

Spelling in the texts has been modernized. The source(s) for the non-biblical texts remain(s) unknown. Translations of all but one of the biblical texts are from the King James Version of the Bible, while those of all biblical paraphrase texts and non-biblical texts are by the editor. The translation of "Herr, wenn ich nur dich habe" is by the editor because the German represents a mistranslation of the original text, which text is correctly rendered in the King James Bible.

1. Ach lieber Herr

Ach lieber Herr! Ich armer Sünder bin nicht wert, daß du unter mein Dach gehest. Sondern sprich nur ein Wort, so wird meine Seele gesund. (Paraphrase of Matthew 8:8 and Luke 7:6–7)

Ah, dear Lord! I, poor sinner, am not worthy to have thee come under my roof. But only say the word, and my soul shall be healed. (Paraphrase of Matthew 8:8 and Luke 7:6–7)

2. Der Herr ist gerecht

Der Herr ist gerecht in allen seinen Wegen, und heilig in allen seinen Werken. Der Herr ist nahe allen, die ihn anrufen, allen die ihn mit Ernst anrufen. Er tut was die Gottsfürchtigen begehren und höret ihr Schreien und hilft ihnen. Der Herr behütet alle, die ihn lieben und wird vertilgen alle Gottlosen. Mein Mund soll des Herrn Lob singen und alles Fleisch lobe seinen heiligen Namen immer und ewiglich. (Psalm 145:17–21)

The Lord is righteous in all his ways, and holy in all his works. The Lord is nigh unto all them that call upon them, to all that call upon him in truth. He will fulfill the desire of them that fear him: he also will hear their cry, and will save them. The Lord preserveth all them that love him: but all the wicked will he destroy. My mouth shall speak the praise of the Lord: and let all flesh bless his holy name for ever and ever. (Psalm 145:17–21, KJV)

3. Ich bin das Brot

Ich bin das Brot des Lebens. Eure Väter haben Manna gessen in der Wüste und sind gestorben. Ich bin das lebendige Brot, von Himmel kommen. Wer von diesem Brot essen wird, der wird leben in Ewigkeit. Und das Brot, daß ich geben werde, ist mein Fleisch, welches ich geben werde für das leben der Welt. Dies ist das Brot, das vom Himmel kommen ist, nicht wie eure Väter haben Manna gessen in der Wüste und sind gestorben. Wer mein Fleisch isset und trinket mein Blut, der hat das ewige Leben. (John 6:48–51, 54, adapted)

I am the bread of life. Your fathers did eat manna in the wilderness, and are dead. I am the living bread which came down from heaven; if any man eat of this bread, he shall live for ever; and the bread that I will give is my flesh, which I will give for the life of the world. This is the bread which comes down from heaven, not as your fathers ate manna in the wilderness and died. Whoso eateth my flesh, and drinketh my blood, hath eternal life. (John 6:48–51, 54, adapted)

4. Herr, wenn ich nur dich habe

Herr, wenn ich nur dich habe, so frage ich nichts nach Himmel und Erde. Wenn mir gleich Leib und Seel verschmacht, so bist du doch, Gott, allezeit meines Herzens Trost und mein Teil. (Psalm 73: 25–26)

Lord, if only I have thee I will ask nothing of heaven and earth. My heart and my flesh may fail, but thou, God, art the strength of my heart and my portion for ever. (Psalm 73:25–26)

5. Es stehe Gott auf

Es stehe Gott auf, daß seine Feinde zerstreuet werden, und die ihn hassen vor ihm fliehen. Vertreibe sie, wie der Rauch vertrieben wird; wie das Wachs zerschmelzet vom Feuer, so müssen umkommen die Gottlosen vor Gott. Die Gerechten aber müssen sich freuen und fröhlich sein vor Gott, und von Herzen sich freuen. (Psalm 68:2–4)

Let God arise, let his enemies be scattered: let them also that hate him flee before him. As smoke is driven away, so drive them away: as wax melteth before the fire, so let the wicked perish at the presence of God. But let the righteous be glad; let them rejoice before God: let them exceedingly rejoice. (Psalm 68:1–3, KJV)

6. Singet Gott

Singet Gott, lobsinget seinem Namen. Machet Bahn, dem der da sanft herfähret. Er heisset Herr, und freuet euch vor ihm. Der ein Vater ist der Waisen und ein Richter der Witwen. Er ist Gott in seiner heiligen Wohnung. Er heisset Herr. Lobsinget ihm, und freuet euch vor ihm.

Sing to God, sing praises to his name. Make way for him who comes gently. His name is the Lord. Rejoice in him who is a father to the orphan and a judge for the widow. He is God in his holy dwelling. His name is the Lord. Sing praises to him and rejoice in him.

7. Ich bin eine Blume zu Saron

Ich bin eine Blume zu Saron und eine Rose im Tal. Wie eine Rose in den Dornen, so ist meine Freundin unter den Töchtern. Wie ein Apfelbaum unter den wilden Bäumen, so ist mein Freund unter den Söhnen. Ich sitze unter dem Schatten, des ich begehre, und seine Frucht ist meiner Kehlen süß. (Song of Solomon 2:1–3)

I am the rose of Sharon, and the lily of the valleys. As the lily among thorns, so is my love among the daughters. As the apple tree among the trees of the wood, so is my beloved among the sons. I sat down under his shadow with great delight, and his fruit was sweet to my taste. (Song of Solomon 2:1–3, KJV)

8. Ich bin schwarz

Ich bin schwarz, aber gar lieblich. Ihr Töchter Jerusalem! Sehet mich nicht an, daß ich so schwarz bin; denn die Sonne hat mich so verbrannt. (Song of Solomon 1:5–6)

I am black but comely, O ye daughters of Jerusalem. Do not look upon me, because I am black, because the sun hath looked upon me. (Song of Solomon 1:5–6, KJV)

9. Ich weiß, daß der Herr

Ich weiß, daß der Herr Gott ist, und unser Herr vor allen Göttern. Alles was er will, das tut er im Himmel, auf Erden, im Meer, und in allen Tiefen. Er läßt die Wolken aufgehen vom Ende der Erden. Er macht Blitzen samt dem Regen. Er läßt den Wind aus den heimlichen Örtern kommen. Sein Name währet ewiglich, und sein Gedächtnis für und für.

I know that the Lord is God, and our Lord above all gods. All that he desires he does, in heaven, on earth, in the sea, and in all the depths. He causes the clouds to form from the ends of the earth. He makes the lightning and the rain. He causes the wind to come from the secret places. His name will continue eternally, and his remembrance for ever and ever.

10. Ich werde bleiben

Ich werde bleiben wie ein grüner Ölbaum im Hause Gottes. Ich verlasse mich auf Gottes Güte immer und ewiglich. Ich danke Gott, denn er kanns wohl machen. Ich will harren auf seinen Namen, denn seine Heiligen haben Freude daran. (Psalm 52:10–11)

But I am like a green olive tree in the house of God: I trust in the mercy of God for ever and ever. I will praise thee for ever, because thou hast done it: and I will wait on thy name; for it is good before thy saints. (Psalm 52:8–9, KJV)

11. Du großer König

Du großer König, Herr Zebaoth, du Herrscher über alle Welt, laß deine herrliche Stimme schallen, daß man sehe deinen ausgereckten Arm mit zornigem Drohen, und mit Flammen des verzehrenden Feuers, mit Strahlen, mit starkem Regen, und mit Hagel, daß die Gottlosen vertilget werden und die Gerechten sich freuen.

Thou great king, Lord of Sabaoth, thou ruler over all the world: let thy splendid voice sound, so that mankind might see thy outstretched arm with angry threats and with flames of consuming fire, with flashes [of lightning], with heavy rain, and with hail. Thus may the ungodly be destroyed and the righteous rejoice.

12. Kommet her, ihr Völker

Kommet her, ihr Völker, lobet den Herrn unsern Gott, denn er hat sein Reich aufgerichtet. Dasselbige wird er uns stärken, denn es ist sein Werk. Er fähret im Himmel allenthalben vom Anbegin. Er zerstreuet die Völker, die da gerne kriegen. Er gibt seinem Donner Kraft, für ihn bebet die Erde, und seine Macht ist in den Wolken. Er ist wundersam in seinem Heiligtum. Preiset und rühmet ihn ewiglich. Alleluja.

Come hither, ye people. Praise the Lord our God, for he hath established his kingdom. The same will he strengthen for us, for it is his work. He rode throughout heaven from the beginning. He scattereth the peoples who love to fight. He giveth power to his thunder, for him the earth doth shake, and his power is in the clouds. He is wonderful in his holiness. Praise and exalt him for ever. Alleluia.

13. Anima mea

Anima mea in æterna dulcedine liquefacta quiescit, o melliflue mi Jesu! O dulcissime mi Jesu! O amantissime mi Jesu! Ecce exultabo lætabor et gloriabor tibi psallam quotidie, cum canticis et fidibus et citharis sonantibus. In te gaudeat cor meum. O amor, o vita, o dulcedo mea. O dulcissime mi Jesu! Amen.

My soul rests, melted in eternal sweetness, o my Jesus, sweet as honey! O my most sweet Jesus! O my most beloved Jesus! Behold, I will daily exult, praise, and glory in thee with the singing of Psalms, with songs and string instruments and the sounding kithara. In thee my heart rejoices. O my Love, my Life, my sweetness. O my most sweet Jesus! Amen.

14. Clamavi

Clamavi in toto corde meo: exaudi me, Domine; justificationes tuas requiram. Clamavi ad te, salvum me fac, ut custodiam mandata tua. Præveni in maturitate, et clamavi; quia in verba tua supersperavi. Prævenerunt oculi mei ad te diluculo, ut meditarer eloquia tua. Vocem meam audi secundum misericordiam tuam, Domine, et secundum judicium tuum vivifica me. Appropinquaverunt persequentes me inique, a lege autem tua longe facti sunt. Prope es tu, Domine, et omnes viæ tuæ veritas. Initio cognovi de testimoniis tuis, quia in æternum fundasti ea. (Psalm 119:145–52 [Vulgate Psalm 118])

I cried with my whole heart; hear me, O Lord: I will keep thy statutes. I cried unto thee; save me, and I shall keep thy testimonies. I prevented the dawning of the morning, and cried: I hoped in thy word. Mine eyes prevent the night watches, that I might meditate in thy word. Hear my voice according unto thy lovingkindness: O Lord, quicken me according to thy judgment. They draw nigh that follow after mischief: they are far from thy law. Thou art near, O Lord; and all thy commandments are truth. Concerning thy testimonies, I have known of old that thou hast founded them for ever. (Psalm 119:145–52, KJV)

15. Dulcis amor

Dulcis amor, Jesu, dulce bonum dilecte mi, sagittis tuis confige me, moriar pro te. Ah mi Jesu, trahe me post te. Langueo pro te, tu lux, tu sol, tu fons, tu spes, tu vita, tu bonitas infinita.

Sweet love, Jesus, sweet goodness, my beloved: let thy arrows pierce me, I will die for thee. Ah my Jesus, draw me after thee. I languish for thee, thou light, thou sun, thou font, thou hope, thou life, thou infinite goodness.

16. Præparate

Præparate corda vestra Domino et servite illi soli. Et liberabit vos de manibus inimicorum vestrorum. Convertimini ad eum, in toto corde vestro, et auferte Deos alienos de medio vestri. (Paraphrase of I Samuel 7:3)

Prepare your hearts for the Lord and serve him alone. And he will deliver you from the hand of your enemies. Return to him with all your heart, and banish foreign gods from your midst. (Paraphrase of I Samuel 7:3)

17. Ad te suspiro

Ad te suspiro, te desidero, o mi Jesu, amor meus et vita mea! Veni, saucia, cor meum, amoris tui jaculo. Ad te accedo, o mi Jesu! Te deprecor, summa bonitas, immensa Caritas. Trahe post te cor meum, ut te solum sequar tibi soli adhæream. Ad te curro, o mi Jesu! Ad te propero, mira suavitas, infinita benignitas, succurre, animæ meæ, amore tuo languenti. O dulcissime Domine, intra vulnera tua vivere cupio. Amplexus tuus sapit ita dulciter, simile mihi essent corda liquescerent velociter. Moriar mundo ut tibi soli vivere possim. Cara Deitas, vera divinitas, pulchra humanitas, immensa bonitas. Maneas in me, ut ego semper maneam in te. Totum cor meum posside, ut in æternum fruar delitiosa tui contemplatione.

For thee I sigh, thee I desire, o my Jesus, my love and my life! Come, my heart, wounded by the dart of thy love. I approach thee, o my Jesus! To thee I pray, ultimate goodness, great love. Draw my heart after thee, so that I would follow thee alone, cling only to thee. To thee I run, o my Jesus! To thee I hasten, wonderful sweetness, infinite goodness; succor with your love my languishing spirit. O most sweet Lord, I desire to live within thy wounds. Thy loving embrace tastes so sweet that my heart liquifies instantly. I die to the world and would live only to thee. Dear God, true divinity, beautiful humanity, immense goodness. Remain in me, and I will ever remain in thee. Be master of my whole heart, as in eternity I would enjoy the delight of contemplating thee.

18. Paratum cor meum

Paratum cor meum, Deus. Cantabo et psalmum dicam. Exsurge, gloria mea. Exsurge, psalterium et cithara. Exsurgam diluculo. Confitebor tibi in populis, Domine, psalmum dicam tibi in gentibus. Quoniam magnificata est usque ad cælos misericordia tua, et usque ad nubes veritas tua. Alleluja. (Psalm 108:2–5 [Vulgate Psalm 107])

O God, my heart is fixed; I will sing and give praise. Awake, my glory. Awake, psaltery and harp: I myself will awake early. I will praise thee, O Lord, among the people: and I will sing praises unto thee among the nations. For thy mercy is great above the heavens: and thy truth reacheth unto the clouds. Alleluia. (Psalm 108:1–4, KJV, adapted.)

Plate 1. Samuel Capricornus, *Geistliche Harmonien III* (Stuttgart, 1664), title page, vox prima partbook. Courtesy of the Marienbibliothek, Halle.

Plate 2. Samuel Capricornus, *Geistliche Harmonien III* (Stuttgart, 1664),
"Ich bin eine Blume zu Saron," vox prima partbook.
Courtesy of the Marienbibliothek, Halle.

Plate 3. Samuel Capricornus, *Geistliche Harmonien III* (Stuttgart, 1664),
"Ich bin eine Blume zu Saron," bassus pro organo partbook.
Courtesy of the Marienbibliothek, Halle.

GEISTLICHE HARMONIEN III

Preface

Dem Durchläuchtigsten Fürsten und Herrn
Herrn Friderichen
Marggrafen zu Baden und Hochberg
Landgrafen zu Susenberg
Grafen zu Spanheim und Eberstein
Herrn zu Röteln, Badenweyler, Lohr und Mahlberg, etc.
Meinem Gnädigsten Fürsten und Herrn, etc.

Durchläuchtigster Gnädigster Fürst und Herr, etc.

Es ist die Music von denen Alten nicht unbillich gleichsam ein Spiel oder Kurtzweil deß Gemüthes und Beruhigung deß von allerhand wichtigen Sorgen angefochtenen Hertzens genennet und gehalten worden. Dann nächst deme, daß durch selbige zuforderst GOTT der Schöpffer aller Dinge, dessen fürtreffliche Gabe sie ist, gelobet und gepriesen wird, ist sie auch ein herrlich Mittel denen schwehrmütigen Gedancken zu begegnen, und die Trawrigkeit auß dem Hertzen zu jagen. Dahero dann je und je, besonders unter **hohen Häuptern** gewesen, und noch sind, die dise Kunst nicht alleine werth halten und lieben, sondern auch (wie es die Erfahrung auch mitten in disen trübseligen Zeiten erweiset) sich mit allem Fleiß angelegen seyn lassen, solche fortzupflantzen, und für Abgang zu bewahren. Was **E. Fürstl. Durchl.** Ihres theils bißhero in Beförderung dererselben hochlöblichst gethan, und wie grosse Zuneigung **Sie** zur selbigen haben hervor blicken lassen, ist männiglich bekandt, und dahero ohne Noth viel hiervon, weil die Sach am Tage, zu gedencken; Zumahlen ich auch viel zu schwach mich befinde, solches der Welt nach genüge für Augen zu stellen.

To the Most Serene Prince and Lord,
Lord Frederick,
Margrave of Baden and Hochberg,
Landgrave of Susenberg,
Count of Spanheim and Eberstein,
Lord of Röteln, Badenweyler, Lohr, and Mahlberg, etc.,
my most gracious Prince and Lord, etc.

Most Serene, Gracious Prince and Lord, etc.

Music was called and thought by the ancients to be, not without reason, like a game or amusement of the soul and a comfort to the heart troubled by all sorts of important cares. For in addition to the fact that through it most importantly God, whose admirable gift it is, is praised and glorified, it is also a splendid means of assuaging heavy thoughts and chasing away sadness from the heart. Therefore it has been and continues to be more and more propagated and kept from decline, especially by High Heads [of State] who not only value and love this art but also (as experience shows us even in these troubled times) apply all industry to this task. What Your Most Princely and Serene Highness has for your part done up to now in most praiseworthy fashion to advance this art and the great affinity you have shown toward it is well known, and therefore, because it is well known, need not be remembered at length here. Furthermore, I find myself unable to demonstrate it sufficiently well to the world.

Alldieweilen ich aber, durch unterschiedliches Ersuchen gegenwärtigen Dritten Theil Geistlicher Harmonien in offentlichen Druck zu geben bewogen, bald Anfangs, da die erste Hand angelegt worden, mich in Erwegung obangeregter *Motiv*, entschlossen, unter **E. Fürstl. Durchl.** hohen Namen denselben außgehen zu lassen; Als habe auch diß Vorhaben keines wegs ändern, sondern solch geringe Wercklein in gebührender Demuth **E. Fürstl. Durchl.** hiemit zuschreiben wollen, unterthänigst bittende, **E. Fürstl. Durchl.** geruhen es gnädigst auff- und anzunehmen, und mit hoher fürstl. Gnade und Huld mir beharrlich zugethan zu verbleiben.

Der allerhöchste GOtt solle **E. Fürstl. Durchl.** sambt Dero gantzem Hoch-Fürstl. Stammen bey hohem Auffnehmen erhalten, und alle erwünschte Wolfarth mildiglich verleyhen.

E. Fürstl. Durchl.

Stuttgart den 30. Martij
    Anno 1664
            unterthänigster
            Samuel Capricornus.

Because I was prompted by various requests to bring out in print the present third part of my Geistliche Harmonien, I decided as soon as I had begun the work to publish it for the above reasons under Your Most Princely and Serene Highness's name. I have had no desire to alter this intention in any way, rather I now wish to inscribe this little work to Your Most Princely and Serene Highness with all due humility, asking most obediently that your Most Princely and Serene Highness deign most graciously to accept it and with high princely grace and honor to remain favorable toward me.

May the almighty God preserve Your Most Princely and Serene Highness along with the entire Princely family in all important endeavors and generously grant all desirable prosperity.

Your Most Princely and Serene Highness's

Stuttgart, 30 March
  in the year 1664
            most obedient
            Samuel Capricornus

1. Ach lieber Herr

Ach   lie-

Ach   lie-   -   ber   Herr!

Ich ar-mer Sün- der,   ich ar-mer

[6]   [6]   ♭   [6]   6

-        ber   Herr!   Ich ar-mer Sün-   der,   ich ar-mer

Ich ar-mer Sün- der,   ich ar-mer Sün- der,

Sün-der, ich ar-mer Sün- der bin   nicht wert,   Ach   lie-

6   6   #   #   #   5 6   [6]   [6]   [6]
                                    [♮]

2. Der Herr ist gerecht

Ernst an- ru- fen, al- - len, die

4 3 [5♭] [♭] [♮] [♭] [6] [♭] [6]

Er tut was die Gotts- fürch- ti- gen be-geh-

ihn __ mit __ Ernst, mit Ernst an- ru- fen.

[♮] ♭ 6 4 3♮ [♮] ♭ [6] [♭] ♭ 4 3♮

24

26

32

3. Ich bin das Brot

und sind ge-stor- ben, und sind ge- stor- ben.

und sind ge-stor- ben, und sind ge-stor- ben.

sind ge-stor- ben, und sind ge-stor- ben, und sind ge-stor- ben.

Ich bin das le-ben- di-ge Brot, vom Him-mel kom-

42

4. Herr, wenn ich nur dich habe

so fra-ge ich nichts nach Him- mel und Er- de, so fra-ge ich nichts nach Him- mel und

7   8 #   #   5   6

Herr,   wenn ich nur dich ha-   be,

Herr,   wenn ich nur dich ha-   be,

Er-   de,   Herr, _____ wenn ich nur dich

4 3   7   3   7   6   6   5[♭]

46

5. Es stehe Gott auf

54

Es ste- he Gott

[6]   [6]   [6]   4 3

Es ste- he Gott auf,   es

Es ste- he Gott

auf,   es ste- he Gott auf, daß sei- ne _Fein- de zer-streu-et wer- den,

[6]

be sie,   wie der Rauch _____ ver- trie- ben wird,

ver- trei-   be sie,   wie der Rauch _____

ver-trie- ben wird;

wie das

wie das

und fröh- lich sein, und fröh- lich, fröh- lich sein vor Gott, und von Her- zen sich

Gott, und fröh- lich sein vor Gott, und fröh- lich sein vor Gott,

sein, und fröh- lich sein vor Gott, und fröh-lich sein vor Gott,

freu- en, und von Her- zen sich freu- en,

und von Her- zen sich freu- en,

und von Her- zen sich

66

6. Singet Gott

Sin- get, sin- get Gott, lob- sin- get sei- nem Na- men,

Sin- get, sin- get Gott, lob- sin- get sei- nem Na-

-sin- get ihm, lob- sin- get, lob- sin- get ihm,

-sin- get ihm, lob- sin- get, lob- sin- get ihm, und freu-

-sin- get ihm, lob- sin- get, lob- sin- get ihm,

7   6[♯]   6 7 6 ♯ ♯

und freu-

-et euch vor ihm,

♯   6   4 3♯   ♮   6   6
              5

7. Ich bin eine Blume zu Saron

Ro- se im Tal,

- se im Tal,

- se im Tal, und ei- ne Ro- se, und ei- ne Ro-

4 3   [6]   [6]   [6] # [6]

und ei- ne Ro-

und ei- ne Ro- se,

- se, und ei- ne Ro- se im Tal, und ei- ne Ro-

6 7 6 #   [6]   [6]

Ro- se in den Dor- nen, so ist mei- ne Freun-

-se, ei- ne Ro- se in den Dor- nen, so ist mei- ne Freun-

ei- ne Ro- se in den Dor- nen, so ist mei- ne

[6]   #   6   # # #   6
        5   [♮]

- din, mei- ne Freun- - din un- ter den Töch- tern,

- din, mei- ne Freun- - din un- ter den Töch- tern,

Freun- din, mei- ne Freun- din un- ter den Töch- tern, so ist mei- ne

        ♭   6   [6]   7 6   4 3
                                       5

57
so ist mei- ne
Freun- din, mei- ne Freun- din un- ter den Töch- tern,
[♯] [6] [♭] 7 6 ♯
60
so ist mei-ne Freun- - din, so ist mei-ne Freun-
Freun- - din, so ist mei-ne
so ist mei-ne Freun- - din, so ist mei-ne
[6] [6] [6]

wie ein Ap- fel-baum un- ter den wil-den Bäu- men,

so _ ist mein _ Freund, so _ ist mein _ Freund, so _ ist mein _ Freund un- ter den Söh- nen,

98

und sei- ne Frucht ist mei- - ner Keh- len süß,

4 3 ♯ 5 ♯ 4 3♯ [♯]

101

und sei- ne Frucht ist

und sei- ne Frucht ist mei-

[♭] 4 3 [♮]

mei- ner Keh- len süß, ist mei- ner Keh- len

ner Keh- len süß,

und sei- ne Frucht ist mei- ner

süß, und sei- ne Frucht ist mei- ner, ist

und sei- ne Frucht ist mei- ner Keh- len süß, ist mei-

Keh- len süß, und sei- ne Frucht ist mei-

6   6   [6]

[♮]

-re, des ich be-geh- re, und sei- ne _

-re, des ich be-geh- re, und sei- ne _ Frucht ist _ mei- ner Keh- len süß,

-re, des ich be-geh- re,

Frucht ist _ mei- ner Keh- len süß,

und sei- ne _

8. Ich bin schwarz

-lich, a- - - ber gar lieb- lich,

ich bin schwarz, ich bin schwarz, a- -

- ber gar lieb- lich, gar lieb- lich, a- ber gar lieb- lich, gar lieb- lich.

Sonata

so schwarz, schwarz, schwarz bin,

se- het mich nicht an, se- het mich nicht an, daß ich

so schwarz, schwarz, schwarz bin, denn die Son-

- ne hat mich so ver-brannt, se- het mich nicht

an, se- het mich nicht an, daß ich so schwarz, schwarz, schwarz bin, denn die Son-

- ne hat mich so ver-brannt, denn die Son-

114

9. Ich weiß, daß der Herr

116

Him- mel, auf Er- den, im Meer, im Him- mel, auf Er- den, im Meer, und in al-

- - - - len Tie- fen.

Ritornello

Vn. 1

Vn. 2

Bn.

B.c.

Er läßt die Wol-ken auf- ge- - hen vom En- de der Er- den,

Er läßt die Wol-ken auf- geh-

10. Ich werde bleiben

grü- ner Öl- baum, ich wer- de blei- ben wie ein _

grü- ner Öl- baum im Hau- - se, im Hau- se, im Hau- - se Got-

Ich ver- las- se mich, ich ver-

Ich ver- las- - se mich, ich ver- las- - se mich

Ich dan- ke, ich dan- - ke, ich dan- - ke

[6]   [6]   3♯ 4   3♯

Gott,   denn er kanns wohl ma- -

♯   [6♮]   [6] [6] 3♮   4

chen, denn er kanns wohl ma-

-chen.

Solo

Ich will har- ren auf sei- nen Na-

Ich will har- ren auf sei- nen Na-

Ich will har- ren auf sei- nen Na-

11. Du großer König

12. Kommet her, ihr Völker

Er fäh - - ret im Him-mel al- lent-

ger- ne krie- gen.

6 4 3   [6]   6 7 6   ♯

-hal- ben, al- lent- hal- ben vom An- be- gin, al- lent- hal- ben, al- lent- hal- ben, al- lent-

4 3   [6]   [♯]   [5♯]

81

und sei- ne Macht ist in den Wol- ken,

- ne Macht ist in den Wol- ken, und sei- ne Macht, und sei- ne

und sei- ne Macht ist

4 3♯ ♯ ♯ 6 6

84

und sei- ne Macht _____ ist in den Wol- ken. Er ist wun- der-

Macht ist in den Wol- ken, ist in den Wol- ken. Er ist wun- der-sam, ist

in den Wol- ken, und sei- ne Macht ist in den Wol- ken. Er ist wun- der-sam, ist

[6] 6 [6] 4 3 6
[5]

13. Anima mea

14. Clamavi

15. Dulcis amor

spes, tu vi- ta, tu lux, tu sol, tu fons, tu spes, tu vi- ta, tu bo- ni-

tu spes, tu vi- ta, tu lux, tu sol, tu fons, tu spes, tu vi- ta, tu bo- ni-

fons, tu spes, tu vi- ta, tu lux, tu sol, tu fons, tu spes, tu vi- ta, tu

-tas, tu bo- ni- tas in- fi- ni- ta, tu bo- ni- tas in- fi- ni- ta.

-tas, tu bo- ni- tas in- fi- ni- ta, tu bo- ni- tas in- fi- ni- ta.

bo- ni- tas in- fi- ni- ta, tu bo- ni- tas, bo- ni- tas in- fi- ni- ta.

16. Præparate

-vi- te, et _ ser- vi- te, et _ ser- vi- te il- li so- li, et _ ser- vi- te il- li so- li.

-vi- te, et _ ser- vi- te, et _ ser- vi- te il- li so- li, et _ ser- vi- te il- li so- li.

et _ ser- vi- te, et ser- vi- te il- li so- li, et ser- vi- te il- li so- li.

Cn.

Vn.

A

T

Et li- be- ra- bit vos de ma- ni- bus i- ni- mi- co-

B

Trb.

B.c.

-rum ve- stro- rum, i- ni- mi- co- rum ve- stro- rum.

-stro- rum, i- ni- mi- co- rum, i- ni- mi- co- rum ve- stro- rum.

-rum ve- stro- rum, i- ni- mi- co- rum ve- stro- rum.

4   3   [6]   4   3♯   ♯

Con- ver- ti- mi- ni, con- ver- ti- mi- ni ad e- um, in to- to cor-

vos de ma- ni- bus, de ma- ni- bus i- ni- mi- co- rum, i- ni- mi- co-

vos de ma- ni- bus i- ni- mi- co- rum ve- stro- rum, i- ni- mi- co- rum ve-

- - bit vos de ma- ni- bus i- ni- mi- co-

[6]

-rum ve- stro- rum, i- ni- mi- co- rum ve- stro- rum.

-stro- rum, i- ni- mi- co- rum, i- ni- mi- co- rum ve- stro- rum.

-rum ve- stro- rum, i- ni- mi- co- rum ve- stro- rum.

4 3 [6] 4 3♯ [♯]

17. Ad te suspiro

18. Paratum cor meum

Cornetto

Soprano 1

Soprano 2

Bass

Pa- ra- tum, pa- ra- tum, pa- ra- tum cor me- um, De- us, pa-ra- tum cor me- um, cor me- um,

Basso continuo

De- us, pa- ra- tum, pa- ra- tum cor me- um,

pa- ra- tum, pa- ra- tum, pa- ra- tum cor me- um, pa- ra- tum cor me- um, pa- ra- tum, pa-

-ra- tum cor me-um, De- us, pa-

-ra- tum, pa-ra- tum cor me-um, pa-ra- tum cor me- um, De- us,

ex- sur- ge, ex- sur- ge, ex- sur- ge,

ex- sur- ge, glo- - ri- a, glo- -

Critical Report

Source

Geistliche Harmonien III (1664) is the sixth of the seven published collections of sacred vocal music to appear during the composer's lifetime. In the four years preceding its publication Capricornus had offered to the public no new sacred music but had instead composed an opera (*Raptus Proserpinae*, 1662), of which only the libretto survives, and had published a volume of instrumental music (*Jocoserium musicalium*, 1663) which is now lost. Nothing is known with certainty of the date of composition of any of the works in *Geistliche Harmonien III*, but it is probably safe to assume that they were all, or nearly all, composed in Stuttgart and thus between 1657 and 1664. The composer chose as dedicatee Friedrich VI, margrave of nearby Baden-Durlach, whose mother was the duchess Barbara von Württemberg. Friedrich, who ruled from 1659 until his death in 1677, is remembered as an enlightened ruler who took an active interest in humanism and the arts but who was forced to spend most of his life in military service as a result of the Thirty Years' War and later battles with the Turks and the French.[1]

Three complete sets of partbooks exist today: RISM lists one in the Stadt- und Universitätsbibliothek Frankfurt and a second in the Marienbibliothek, Halle. A third, formerly in Berlin, now resides in Krakow under its Berlin shelf number, Mus. ant. prat. C 223. Various libraries also possess incomplete sets of partbooks, including the Württemburgische Landesbibliothek, Stuttgart; the Universitätsbibliothek, Tübingen; the Sächsische Landesbibliothek, Dresden; and the British Library, London. This source situation implies a relatively wide distribution for *Geistliche Harmonien III*, although the scarcity of complete sets also implies a lack of continuing interest as the centuries progressed. The present edition was made from the microfilm of the Halle partbooks housed in the Deutsches Musikgeschichtliches Archiv, Kassel, and from selected pages of the Frankfurt partbooks.

Capricornus's original was set in movable type and published by Johann Weyrich Rösslin the younger, the official printer of the Württemberg court.[2] Rösslin learned his trade with Endter in Nuremberg. His father, J. W. Rösslin the elder, had served similarly as court printer until 1644, when as a result of the war, business fell off precipitously. The younger Rösslin issued a large number of publications (not principally music) between 1649 and his death in 1684.

Editorial Practice

Note Values

The original note values have been retained in all cases. The relationship between duple and triple meter is that familiar to performers of sixteenth- and early seventeenth-century music: one semibreve of duple meter equals three semibreves of triple.

Barlines

In the original partbooks barlines are found only in the basso continuo part, where they are placed every breve, with an occasional instance of two barlines per breve or two breves per barline. This original barring produces a $\frac{4}{2}$ time signature, which is the signature of choice for late sixteenth-century music, based as it is to a great extent on semibreves (whole notes) and minims (half notes) with an occasional pair or run of quarter notes. Mid-seventeenth-century style, however, makes considerable use of quarters, eighths, and even sixteenth notes, so that such a barring creates inordinately long measures that make counting difficult. (In this regard, it is interesting that at some point a violinist added small hashmarks every semibreve in one of the violin partbooks from the Frankfurt set.) I am unable to perceive any significant relationship between the original barring and the composer's intended grouping of notes. Their purpose seems merely to give the basso continuo player some kind of regular benchmark for keeping the ensemble together. For example, in the last few measures of "Ad te suspiro" the original print maintains breve-by-breve barring even though it masks the final hemiola (i.e., barlines appear at the beginnings of the present measures 139, 141, and 143). In only one instance, the $\frac{6}{8}$ concluding section of "Ich bin schwarz," has the original barring been left unchanged. Capricornus's original time signatures have been retained, since their use combined with more-frequent barring produces a notational look quite like our modern one and apparently quite in keeping with performances of Capricornus's day. In summary: the present edition places barlines every semibreve in duple meter and every three semibreves in triple.

Accidentals

Because only the basso continuo partbook contains barlines, the modern convention according to which an accidental remains valid until it is canceled either by another accidental or by a barline does not pertain in the original. More particularly, one cannot always be certain when a given notated accidental has lost its validity, since frequently the sharp or flat sign is not repeated when only one or two notes intervene before the affected note is restruck. For instances without ambiguity, the present edition follows modern convention, according to which a given accidental, once it has been notated, need not be renotated until the following measure. Where ambiguity exists, I offer my best guess with a notated accidental above the staff. Any accidental preceding a note on the staff is original; any above the note is editorial.

For the most part, *Geistliche Harmonien III* conforms to standard seventeenth-century practice in its use of the sharp and flat accidental signs only, without the natural sign. The few natural signs that are to be found in the original print, all in "Ich werde bleiben," have been reported in the critical notes to that piece. Therefore, all other natural signs in this edition, including those in the figured bass, are the result of adopting modern conventions for their use.

Beaming

Because the original was typeset, it has no beaming. In the absence of an original beaming to indicate the composer's intentions concerning phrasing or grouping of notes, the present edition employs standard patterns of beaming. As was the case with barlines, the performer should take this as a notational convention for the sake of facilitating rehearsals and performance, not as an indication of Capricornus's intended grouping or articulation of melodic lines.

Text Underlay

The absence of beaming in the original left Rösslin's typesetter to choose another method for indicating text underlay in melismatic passages. This was done using slurs, but in a rather inconsistent, not to say haphazard, manner. That is, the intended text underlay is invariably clear, but it is notated sometimes with slurs, sometimes without (i.e., simply through placement of the syllable under the appropriate note). Although I perceive no interpretative significance in the presence or absence of slurs for indicating text, the original slurring is retained just in case some sort of significance might later be discovered to attach to them. In the end, the only context in which text setting is anything other than standard and predictable is in the 8-7-8 cadence formula, where the second of two syllables is sometimes sounded with the last note, sometimes with the second (see "Der Herr ist gerecht," mm. 65–66 and 68–69, tenor). The source is quite clear about how all of these should be handled (if inconsistent from one to the next).

These are given in the present edition exactly as they appear in the original.

Slurs

Slurs not related to text setting appear occasionally (see "Ach lieber Herr," mm. 41–42 and 45–46, violin parts). These have also been retained in the edition.

Fermatas

The source supplies fermatas inconsistently. That is, the end of a section frequently brings a fermata in some but not all of the parts. This appears to be almost certainly the result of carelessness in typesetting and has no significance for the performance of the music. In any context where all parts come to a cadence point simultaneously and at least one part carries a fermata, all parts are given a fermata in this edition.

Repeated Sections

Several of the pieces have final sections that are repeated. In each case, the last chord appears twice in the original, i.e., as unlabeled first and second endings. The first appearance as it is appears in the present edition; the second, after the repeat sign, is the same chord notated in longs with fermatas. Such notation seems unnecessarily clumsy, since any performer accustomed to the baroque notation of da capo arias will be familiar with the concept of ignoring the fermata on the first pass through. In the present edition the performer should likewise understand that the fermatas apply only to the repeat of the section.

Other Issues

Arabic numbers have been added to the titles of the works. Voice names have been given in English. The indication for a trill in the source is "t." but this has been set with the familiar modern symbol. The notation of slurs and ties has been regularized according to modern conventions. The placements of dynamics and clefs have also been regularized. The text of the underlay has been edited for clarity with regard to capitalization and punctuation.

Critical Notes

The voices and instruments are abbreviated as follows: S = Soprano; A = Alto; T = Tenor; B = Bass; Vn. = Violin; Va. = Viola; Gamba = Viola da gamba; Cn. = Cornetto; Rec. = Recorder; Trb. = Trombone; Bn. = Bassoon; B.c. = Basso continuo. Reports of accidentals reflect the notation of the source (with its use of flats and sharps in place of natural signs). Pitches are designated according to the system in which middle C = c'.

1. Ach lieber Herr

Mm. 75–78, B.c., clef is baritone (C5) but should be tenor (C4).

2. Der Herr ist gerecht

M. 1, Vn. 2, time signature is 𝄴 ³⁄₂. Mm. 1–13, Vn. 2, pattern of rests is one dotted breve too short. M. 17, B, note 2 has ♭. M. 94, A, quarter rest is lacking. M. 140, B.c., note lacks dot.

3. Ich bin das Brot

M. 16, B.c., figure "6" is attached to note 2 (rather than note 1). M. 19, T, note 1 is dotted eighth note. M. 57, B.c., figures "4 3" are attached to note 2 (rather than note 3). M. 66, Vn. 1, first rest is quarter rest. M. 67, Vn. 1, note 2 is b♭". Mm. 77–78, T, syllables "-ket mein Blut" are shifted one note to the left. M. 79, B.c., figure "7" is attached to note 2 (rather than note 3). M. 83, Vn. 1, note 4 is eighth note. M. 83, T, note 3 is b♭. M. 83, B, quarter rest is lacking. M. 86, vn. 1, pattern of rests is half, eighth, half. M. 89, Vn. 1, note 3 is whole note.

4. Herr, wenn ich nur dich habe

M. 19, B.c., figures "4 3♯" are attached to note 3 (rather than m. 20, note 1). Mm. 22–26, T1, pattern of rests is one dotted breve too short. M. 51, B.c., note 2, top numeral in first figure is 3. Mm. 55–56, Vn. 2, breve rest is lacking.

5. Es stehe Gott auf

M. 39, Bn., note 3 is b. Mm. 53–78, S2, pattern of rests is one whole too short. M. 98, Vn. 1, second rest is quarter rest. M. 110, S2, notes 2 and 4 are eighth notes.

6. Singet Gott

M. 3, B.c., note 2, figures are 3♯ 4. Mm. 39–43, Trb., pattern of rests is one dotted half too long. M. 89, S2, note 6 is eighth note. M. 147, S1, dynamic indication is lacking. M. 164, B, note 9 is thirty-second note.

7. Ich bin eine Blume zu Saron

M. 31, Vn. 1, note 2 is sixteenth note. Mm. 31–34, S, pattern of rests is one half rest too short. M. 32, T, note 7 is sixteenth note. Mm. 41–43, S, pattern of rests is one whole too short. M. 53, S, note 7 is sixteenth note. M. 58, T, notes 6–11 are missing on microfilm and are supplied by editor. M. 60, T, rest is lacking. M. 71, S, note 3 is dotted sixteenth note. M. 74, B.c., figures "4 3" are attached to note 5 (rather than note 6). M. 84, B.c., note 1, figures are ⁷₍♯₎ 6. M. 93, B.c., note 1 has ♭. Mm. 98–102, S, pattern of rests is one breve too short. M. 104, T, note 6 is eighth note. M. 104, Trb./Gamba, note 7 has ♯. M. 116, S, note 7 is eighth note. M. 126, S, note 4 is eighth note.

8. Ich bin schwarz

Mm. 15–40, all recorders, pattern of rests is one whole too short. M. 60, Rec. 4, time signature is ³⁄₂. M. 60, Rec. 5, time signature is ⁶⁄₈.

9. Ich weiß, daß der Herr

Heading is "Ritornello" in instrumental parts but "Sonata" in vocal parts. M. 11, B.c., figures "6," "4 3♯," and "♯" are shifted one note to the left. Mm. 18–33, Vn. 1, pattern of rests is one breve too long. M. 31, figure "6" is attached to note 1 (rather than note 2). M. 56, B, note 9 is eighth note. M. 58, B.c., entire measure is missing in original and is supplied by editor.

10. Ich werde bleiben

M. 19, Vn. 2, note 4 is eighth note. Mm. 20–28, T, pattern of rests is one half rest too long. Mm. 28–35, S2, pattern of rests is one dotted whole too short. M. 54, trb., second rest is quarter rest. Mm. 68–69, T, pattern of rests is one whole too short. M. 72, B.c., note 1, figures are 3 4; figure "6" is attached to note 3 (rather than note 4). M. 89, Vn. 2, note 2 is thirty-second note. M. 92, T, rest is lacking. M. 95, B.c., note 5, figures are 4 3♯. M. 99, B.c., note 4, figures are 4 3♯. M. 100, Vn. 2, note 2, ♮ is in original. Mm. 106–7, B.c., note 4, ♮ is in original. M. 130, S2, note 4, ♮ is in original. M. 140, Vn. 1, ♮ is in original.

11. Du großer König

M. 25, Vn. 2, quarter rest is lacking. M. 110, B.c., note 3, figures are 6 4. M. 115, Vn. 1, note 5 is e♭".

12. Kommet her, ihr Völker

Mm. 14–17, S, rest is only one breve in length. M. 28, B, note 7 is eighth note. M. 36, B.c., figure "♭" is attached to note 3 (rather than note 2). M. 55, Vn. 1, note 5 has dot. M. 63, B.c., note 4 is c. M. 82, Vn. 1, note 3 is sixteenth note. M. 87, B, note 5 lacks dot. M. 90, B, note 2 is thirty-second note. M. 102, Vn. 2, notes 3–4 are missing in original and are supplied by editor. Mm. 119–24, T, clef is baritone (C5) but should be tenor (C4).

13. Anima mea

M. 5, S, note 3 is e'. M. 26, S, slur extends over notes 1–3. M. 26, T, note 2 is c'. M. 32, B.c., note 2 is g. M. 33, S, note 2 is eighth note. M. 37, S, note 5 is eighth note. M. 38, B, third rest is lacking. M. 40, S, rest is unclear. M. 67, B, note 1 has

♯. M. 81, T, notes 1 and 2 are quarter notes; note 3 has ♮. M. 82, B, note 4 is B. M. 87, B, note 4 is missing in original and is supplied by editor; syllable "-men" is attached to note 3 (rather than note 2); editor has supplied the "Amen" on notes 3–4.

14. Clamavi

Mm. 1–5, A, pattern of rests is two breves too short. M. 11, A, rest is lacking. M. 12, Vn. 2, note 5 (of edition) has dot (rather than note 3). Mm. 21–102, T, clef is baritone (C5) but should be tenor (C4). M. 82, B.c., figure "♯" is attached to note 4 (rather than note 6). M. 83, Vn. 2, note 9 is eighth note. M. 85, vn. 2, note 4 is eighth note. M. 88, A, note 10 is eighth note. M. 97, B.c., figure "6" is attached to note 3 (rather than note 2). M. 102, B.c., note is E.

15. Dulcis amor

Mm. 11–14, S2, pattern of rests is one whole too short. Mm. 43–46, S2, pattern of rests is one half rest too long. M. 76, Va. 1, note 2 has ♯. M. 81, S2, note 3 has ♯ (rather than note 2). M. 98, Va. 2, note 1 is eighth note. M. 102, S2, second rest is quarter rest. M. 107, Bn., note 1 is dotted eighth note. M. 108, B, note 1 is undotted eighth note followed by quarter rest.

16. Præparate

Mm. 11–36, Vn., pattern of rests is one whole too short. M. 18, T, note 2 is e'; note 3 is c'. M. 18, B, note 5 is c'. M. 34, T and B, dynamic indication is lacking. M. 52, Vn., notes 1 and 2 are quarter notes. M. 64, T, note 10 is e'. M. 81, T, notes 5 and 6 are both c'. M. 86, B.c., note lacks dot. M. 97, A, rest is lacking. M. 104, A, note 3 is sixteenth note. M.

104, T, notes 4 and 10 are thirty-second notes. M. 138, B.c., figure "♯" is attached to note 1 (rather than note 2). M. 140, B.c., note 2, figure is ⁵. M. 142, B.c., figures "4 3♯" are attached to note 1 (rather than note 2); figure "♯" is attached to note 2 (rather than m. 143, note 1).

17. Ad te suspiro

M. 3, Va. 3, note 4 is a; note 5 is b. M. 6, Vn. 2, note 4 is thirty-second note. Mm. 6–7, Va. 2, slur extends from m. 6, note 3, to m. 7, note 1. M. 45, B.c., second figure is 3 (rather than 4). M. 57, Va. 1, dynamic indication is lacking. M. 57, B.c., note 5, figure is 6. Mm. 85–144, all viola parts are texted as in vocal parts. Mm. 117–32, Va. 1, pattern of rests is eight dotted wholes too short. M. 126, B.c., note 1, figures are 6 5.

18. Paratum cor meum

M. 10, Cn., note 3 is sixteenth note. M. 10, B.c., figure "6" is attached to note 1 (rather than note 2). M. 11, Cn., notes 11 and 12 are sixteenth notes. M. 28, Cn., note 4 is thirty-second note. Mm. 32–44, Cn., pattern of rests is one whole too short. Mm. 45–76, S2, pattern of rests is one breve too long. M. 56, Cn., notes 3–6 are missing in original and are supplied by editor. M. 57, Cn., notes 1–2 are missing in original and are supplied by editor. Mm. 70–71, B, syllables "-ri-a" are shifted two notes to the right. M. 71, B, syllable "glo-" is shifted three notes to the right. M. 146, B.c., figures "6" and "4 3♯" are shifted one note to the left; an extraneous figure "♯" is attached to note 3. M. 147, B, rest is lacking. M. 156, B.c., ♭ on note 6 is notated as figure instead.

Notes

1. This information is taken from the *Allgemeine deutsche Biographie*, vol. 7 (Munich: Duncker & Humblot, 1875–1912), 461–62.

2. The information on the Rösslin family is taken from Josef Benzing, *Die Buchdrucker des 16. und 17. Jahrhunderts im deutschen Sprachgebiet*, 2nd ed., Beiträge zum Buch- und Bibliothekswesen, no. 12, ed. Max Pauer (Wiesbaden: Otto Harrassowitz, 1982), 456–58.